Receiving and understanding the value of money
allows a child to make a decision. With knowledge
and empowerment a child car soar.

To my mom, Marybeth, who taught
me the value of money, no matter the amount
received. You are my angel.
To Jon, Jeremy, and Steffanie.

Mitchel, you will soar.
Love, Mommy.

Title: Birthday Bucks
Description: First edition. Audience: Ages 4-9. Audience: Preschool – 3. Reading Age: 5-9 years
Summary: Story of an eight year olds birthday introduces children to basic
ideas about money in this accessible picture book about financial literacy.
Subject: Money-Juvenile literature

The artist created the illustrations for this book digitally

Birthday Bucks

Written by
Amy Kalna

Illustrated by
Jasurbek Ruzmat

Family is gathered, with smiles so wide,
To celebrate my birthday, side by side.

Now we'll enjoy my cake with laughter and fun,
Sharing happy moments under the sun.

Lots of presents all around,
Unwrapping them, fun will abound.
The biggest box catches my curious eyes,
I wonder what's inside – it's a big surprise!

A shiny new scooter, just my perfect size,
I can ride and explore under sunny skies!

Next, my eyes sparkle with glee,
A rectangular box catches my curiosity.
Grannie said it was her gift to me,
Pondering thoughts, guessing what it could be.

"Happy Birthday!" Grannie exclaimed.
While she smiled with joy, I complained,
"What can I do with these?"

Grannie responded, "These are Birthday Bucks! How about saving them for a special day?

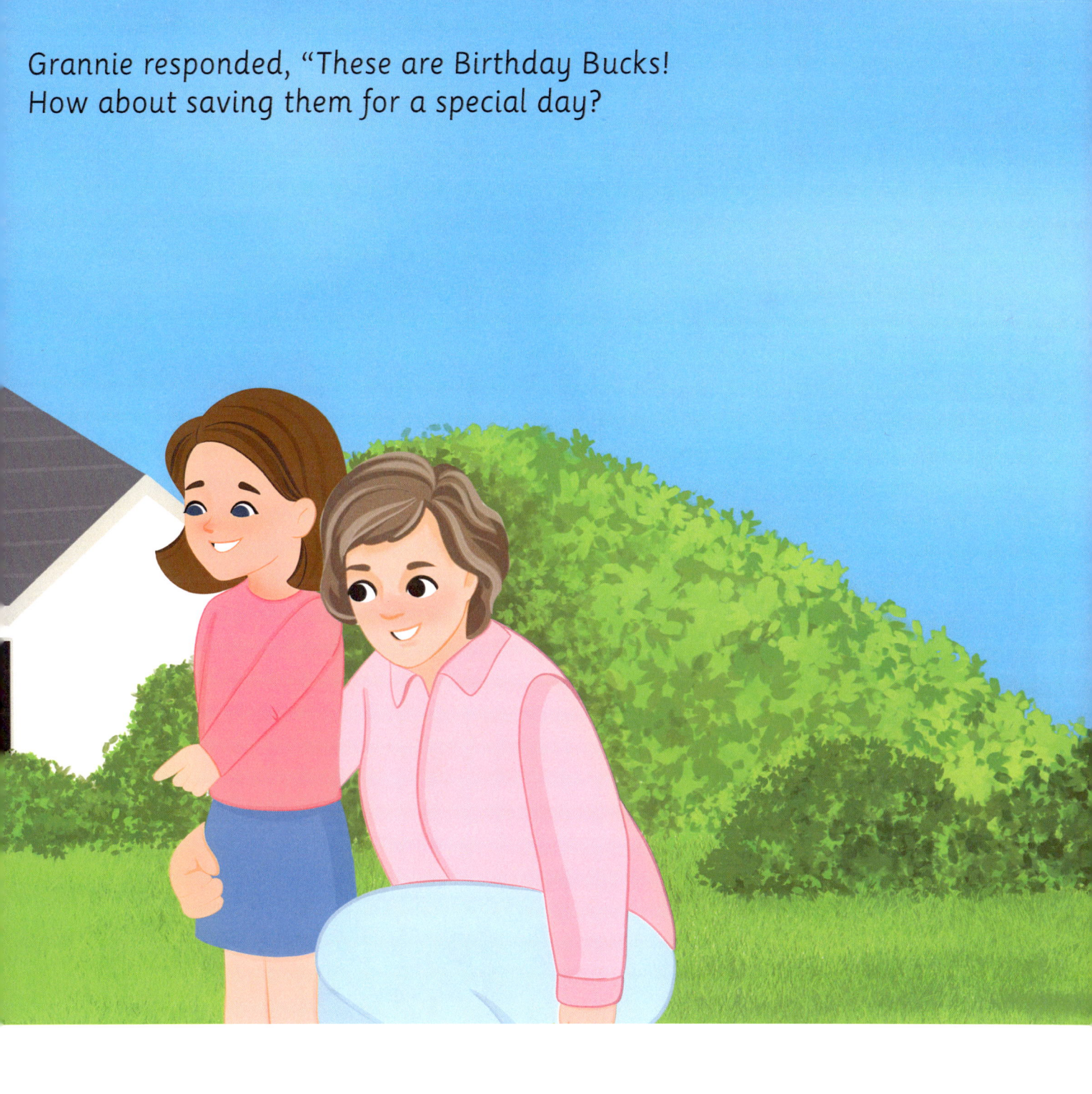

Saving money is really neat,
Let's learn why it's such a treat!

For a future goal or special toy,
Saving money brings so much joy.
You can buy things you've wanted for so long,
With patience and saving, you can't go wrong!"

Mom can take me to a bank,
Doors so heavy, I'll give them a yank.
The bankers will keep it safe, like a treasure chest,
And help it grow, it's the very best!

Coins and bills, I put them inside,
Watching my savings grow with pride.

But Grandpa had a different idea, his eyes full
of cheer, "SPEND the money, my dear,
let your dreams appear.

Spending money is when we use,
Our coins and bills for things we choose.
Spend on things that bring you delight,
Like books, games, or a fancy bike.

A shiny toy may catch your eye,
But think twice before you buy.
Is it something you will use each day,
Or will it soon be put away?"

SPEND

In my hands, bills shuffle with glee,
I'll buy something that lasts, that's the key!

A piñata swings high, swaying in the breeze.
My mom gently reminds me with care,
"You can GIVE the money, and show that you share.

It's part of Philanthropy, a special word,
It's about helping others, haven't you heard?
We can buy toys or lend a hand,
To help the sick or protect the land.

Money can be used to help others in need,
By donating, we do a generous deed."

GIVE

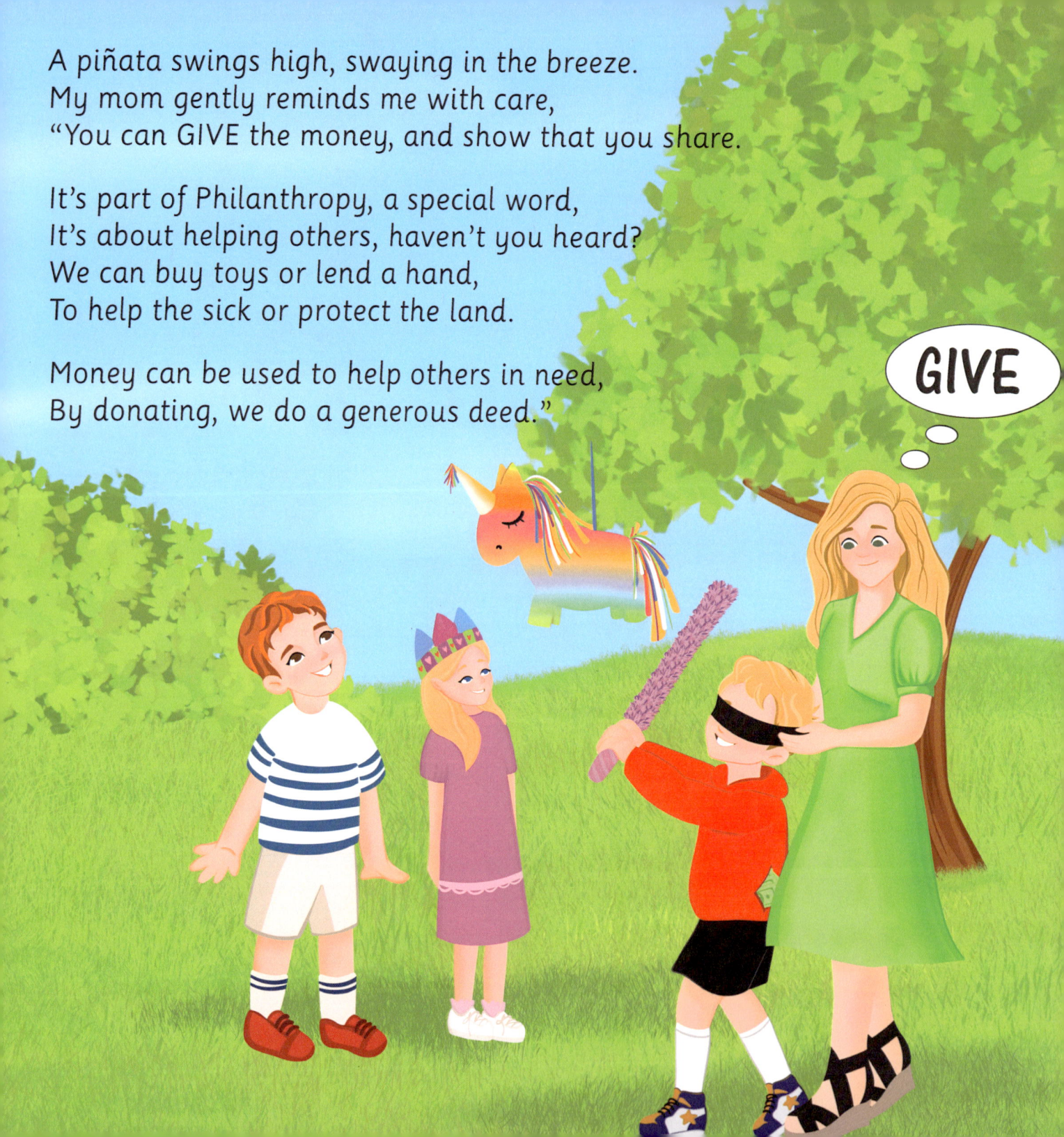

Helping others, making things right,
With a giving heart, everything feels right.

Dad shouts over our giggles, "I know one last way you can use those bucks, INVEST!

Investing money is a special way,
To make it grow and have more someday.
It may be confusing and hard to surmount,
But with help from a
grown-up you can
open an account.

INVEST

Invest in things that grow with time,
like stocks, and bonds, to see their value climb.
As you go along, the value may go down,
But you are resilient, and will stay strong.

Invest in things that you believe,
Watch your money bloom and achieve.
You'll learn and grow with every choice,
Listen to your inner voice."

Thanks Dad! I'll invest some of my bills, watch them rise,
Like magic beans reaching for the skies.
With investing, I can reach for the stars,
Mom always says, "Dream big, no matter who you are."

Thank you, family, for all you do,
Gifting me with a fun birthday, and teaching me too.
I felt empowered, I learned something new,
With these Birthday Bucks, I knew what I could do.

SAVE
Keep and store for use in the future

What can you do with money?

SPEND
Use money to pay for things.
Exchange money for something or a service

BUCKS!
Money

GIVE
Hand over to someone in need or a charitable organization

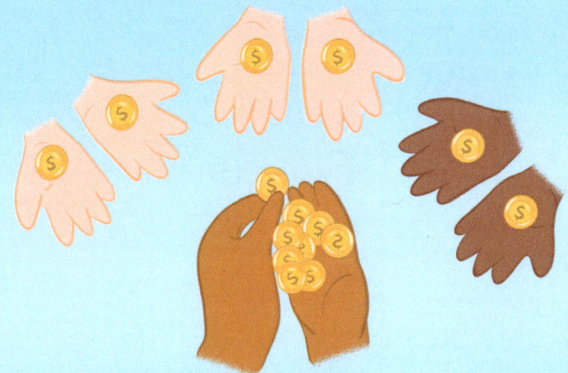

INVEST
Put money into something with the goal of it increasing in value over time